With Best Wishes
to Uncle and Aunty.

Radha Narayan
26 May 1999

THE MELODY OF SILENCE

Radha Narayan

MINERVA PRESS
LONDON
MONTREUX LOS ANGELES SYDNEY

THE MELODY OF SILENCE
Copyright © Radha Narayan 1997

All Rights Reserved

No part of this book may be reproduced in any form,
by photocopying or by any electronic or mechanical means,
including information storage or retrieval systems,
without permission in writing from both the copyright owner
and the publisher of this book.

ISBN 1 86106 229 X

First Published 1997 by
MINERVA PRESS
195 Knightsbridge
London SW7 1RE

Printed in Great Britain by
CPI Ltd, London

THE MELODY OF SILENCE

FOREWORD

This collection of poems, Radha Narayan's first, is a treatise in fluid eloquence, attractive in its simplicity yet thought-provoking in content – an embodiment of deeply philosophical thought and an incisive perception rare in one so young.

The poems reveal an amazing range of thought and a command of language that is, to say the least, prodigious. 'Maybe not in years, but surely in mind' – the young poetess displays a maturity and wisdom beyond her years. The poems, some simple and sweet and some deeply perceptive, are reflections on life which can hold even the wisest of us in good stead on the tumultuous road of life.

> Words are my life;
> My life is words.
> Expressed with beauty
> Yet staying unheard.
>
> My feelings are those of a poet
> Such a heart is mine

says the young poetess, whose poems are indeed 'a spontaneous outflow of innermost feelings'. Beautiful beyond words, thought-provoking and inspiring, this collection of poems strikes a chord somewhere deep, deep inside...

The Melody of Silence is so intense that you can hear little else as you move from one poem to the next.

Dr Afsar Khan
Principal
Embassy of India School
Riyadh
Saudi Arabia

Introduction

This is the first for me,
My first public appearance –
With any luck this may be
My literary entrance.

Firstly I'd like to tell you
Before you proceed
That for me, one thing is true:
I simply love to read.

For me it's an obsession
And a way to spend my time;
I have an absolute passion
For laughter, sense and rhyme.

I think I've mixed a bit of all,
A twenty-four hour hand,
A Reynolds pen and a paper roll.
P.S. Common sense and my mind.

It hardly takes a minute
To write down something memorised,
But it takes quite long to sit,
Imagine, and have words sized.

To me, it's a world of wonder,
The power to express oneself,
To be able to wander
Deep within yourself.

There are more things to life
Than what is plain to see.
There are deeper thoughts to derive,
Different ways to be.

There is more within a mind,
An infinite variety –
Emotions of different kinds
To dwell on silently.

What is peace internally?
What decides our actions?
What is anger really?
What our future sanctions?

Deep questions with improper answers
Always aggravate me.
My poems are mere cures
For my own curiosity.

Contents

Part 1 – Realms of Ecstasy

The Melody of Silence	13
Far Away, In Another Land...	15
Superlatives	16

Part 2 – Minds and Morals

Promise	21
Analytical View	22
To Touch A Star	24
Solitude Is Not Loneliness	26
Spirit	27
Colour of Money – Colour of Discord	28
Growing Up	30
Dreams – Their Reality	31
Grammar – A Complex Sentence	32

Part 3 – Confession

Mystery	35
Wonder After Wonder	37
Unfortunately	39
Mad Desire	41
Paradox	42
Secret	43
In Another's Eyes	45
Decision	47
The Truth At Last	49

Part 4 – A Bit Of Advice

Road To Happiness	53
Simple Advice, Hard to Follow	56
Sadly	58
Absolute Contentment	59
Self-Esteem	60
God Helps Those Who Help Themselves	61
Judge Yourself	62

Part 5 – Eulogy

I Agree, But Not For Me	65
Vision of Loveliness	66
Bapu – An Ideal Idol	69

Part 6 – The Sands of Time

Memories	73
Ten Years From Now	74
Time – A Fleeting Glimpse	76
Pandora and Life	77

Part 7 – Denouement

Writing Poetry	81
Where Words Are Useless	82
It Is Much More	83

Part 8 – Experience 87

Part 1
Realms of Ecstasy

The Melody of Silence

It's a mad, mad world,
But a fantasy no less,
New realms are forever appearing,
There is nobody mortal... all-knowing.
Impossibilities and miracles
Are forever occurring.
Even plain truths
And seemingly inevitable
Things become mere possibilities,
And our own capacities
Are such, we are able
To achieve impossibilities.
There is no such fact
We can always rely on.
Life and death are normal things.
If the soul is eternal, what are human beings?
Time is for ever gone,
Life is full of inexplicable things.

The wonder that is science,
A funny thing it is,
Putting logic where it makes no sense,
Making sense out of nonsense,
Full of meaning, yet meaningless,
When compared to the infinite worlds beyond us.
Nothing material is ours for ever
Yet memories forever encore
Far beyond with a strange symphony,
Bays beyond a shore –
A perfect melody, symbolising harmony.
Time is defined, but even so
It is basically a mere nothing,
For when nothing ever seems to count,
Memories, worries and aspirations amount
To almost nothing,
Pure Silence is all around.

It seems very strange
And I doubt if I can say
Or with words attempt to explain
That as such we feel neither happiness nor pain –
A sweet tune takes us far away,
A tune – The Melody Of Silence.

Far Away, In Another Land...

Beyond fact, past the tiniest truths of fiction,
There lies an immense world to see.
What we feel to be an ocean
Is a droplet in reality.
Even time is not merely a watch,
No watch counts till eternity.
Stars, despite their distance from us,
Endear only proximity.
The infinite colours in a clear sunset
Display such immense variety.
Truly, even our own thoughts wander so far;
A priceless, divine novelty.
My pen cannot describe my feelings
At nature's supremacy,
Neither can music, nor tune
Compose my heart's melody.
If only I could simply watch the world's wonders
In absolute tranquillity.
Far away there is so much more,
So much more to see.

Superlatives

Every poet wishes to bring
Out the moods of all things
Within a span of time,
Yet make it through rhyme.
But would there ever be a mood as such
When no emotion springs;
Nothing seems to account for as much?

Would there ever be a life,
Had we never to strive
To make good our dreams,
And fulfil each whim?
Would there be any happiness that way,
Where we do not have feelings,
And all emotions knock our doors and turn away?

Pain is just a part of happiness and peace,
Mad though it may seem.
For it is only a state of mind;
(Happiness) we leave behind,
And another such state we enter, praying,
That soon the past will be returning,
Such is human nature, forever change resisting.

Life lasts only a little long, and a little short,
For, of the infinite cosmos, we are merely a part.
And, within large, universal limits,
Our life is simply one bit.
Yet every moment we hold on to tightly,
Knowing, and forever remembering,
That every action we make affects us more than slightly.

Within this short span of time,
When our life is at its prime,
Each and every man aspires
To follow his desires,
And in living his dreams, he finds his peace.
But not for one moment realising
Why he has endured the pain and work it took to achieve this.

Of course, one man's emotions cannot the world alter,
Neither can a galaxy falter,
For we are just minute beings,
Within a larger, much larger thing,
Intergalactic and infinite, we can never explain.
But it is a fact that feelings,
Of one man or many, form an important factor of life...

One that for centuries can never be explained
Unless emotions of man and his dreams remain.

Part 2

Minds and Morals

Promise

I am no great star,
I am no perennial river.
I am as direct as a six year old.
And yet as reserved as can be.
I have been there in the world
Before even time began.
And I will stay for ever.

I have seen life,
And I have seen death.
I have been through the universe.
I have seen all there is to see.
No one can describe me exactly in verse,
I am one, I am all,
And yet I am immaterial.

I am the natural first in any person's heart.
I am open to all who wish to know me.
I am trusty, irresponsible, whatever you wish me.
I am varying, yet constant, I have a million ways to be.
Even below Hope I am found.
I am the Spirit.

Analytical View

One of the deepest mysteries
Is the dormant October mind,
The steely cover of the most fascinating
Person one could ever meet;
He is one who can contradict
Anyone and anything.
Even the most positive and logical sounding.

For the logic in his mind
Far exceeds that of the reasoning of others.
Beneath that impermeable cover
Lies a person of a kind.
He is a person of whom no matter what is said,
He will not rest until he proves you wrong,
And none but you is surer.

Nothing ever stands in his way,
He is the soaring eagle, who lives for new horizons.
He knows the secret of existence.
Forever in an impeccable disguise, mystery forms his day.
The rudest insults of others will roll off his back.
He knows himself; his advantages and shortcomings;
And rarely, once in a blue moon, accepts compliments.

No one will ever know him better than himself,
Unless he finds another in which to confide.
He would know the truths behind life and death,
If only he realised the value of the planet behind himself.
He speaks the blunt truth,
Whether to friend or foe.
In that respect he has no emotion to hide.

Behind his steely cover on the outside
Lies a quite different person.
He is passionate; each thing he touches
Becomes something he madly pursues and follows behind.
He has a deep interest
In the phases of life and death:
Religion, philosophy and logic interest this man.

This October-November mind – almost like a myth, dangerous
 thistle
Grows around him, yet has the languid beauty of an intoxicant
Rich, dark, wine-red gentleness
Forms the core of his steely secret mettle.
His invincibility forms his attractiveness
Yet he can resist anything: no mortal influences him...
No man... and no woman.

To Touch A Star

It is a world of bliss I enter,
At heart I am no more
The child who at each step falters
And cries at every sore.
Day after day, and night after night,
I see only one thing,
A faraway beautiful sight;
An enhanced, inspiring being.

My life rests no more with me,
My soul lives far away.
There are more new worlds to see,
New places to stay.
Living by the light and yet in shadow
I see my life ahead,
I simply cannot stop now;
There are things to be said.

New dreams and desires haunt my soul,
Urge is within my heart:
In this world I must play my role,
I must do my part.
I stay by brooks where flowers grow best,
Where unmatched stays the dawn,
My goal is nigh, I cannot rest,
I must go on and on.

I see the sun in majestic glare
Rising by the tides
Yet at my achievements I stare
And constantly chide.
But I can't always keep the pace,
I do stop now and then,
The world is after all a race
Among the best, fleetest men.

I do fall down once or twice
And stumble as I reach,
Yet these only make me wise,
It is success I seek.
Nothing can deter me,
I will win one day,
After all there are new worlds to see,
New places to stay.

Solitude Is Not Loneliness

Oh, Muse of astronomy –
Beloved Urania!
I call now on you
For you are truly
The earnest stargazer's
Wildest dream come true.

To me, you are not merely
A scientific miracle –
Novae and supernovae
Or amateur astronomy's
Mild and gentle
Stars and nebulae.

But to me, even the faint little quasar
Is an extremely significant
Part of the essence
Of my life; as is the unlucky pulsar,
Even that is a relevant
Part of my existence.

But no! I am no great astronomer –
And the great Eyes,
Cepheus and Cassiopeia,
Shining through the epochs and eras
Will tell you the same –
As will Lyra, Perseus and Andromeda.

Spirit

You can take me from a place
That has embraced me for years,
You can take from my world a dear face
And I may break up once into tears.
Then I firmly stand against you yet;
You can never take my spirit.

You may black out the joys in my life,
You may remove the last trace of hope from me.
After reconcilement, I may yet survive.
Angry or unhappy I may be.
But after years of struggle, I will stand erect:
You can never take my spirit.

Colour of Money – Colour of Discord

If ever I have felt this way,
Though I am sure I haven't,
I can say one thing for sure –
It was not in this life, on any day.
An excuse for my feelings I cannot find,
But of them, my mind is sure.

It started at the beginning
Like any story should.
It was when as a kid,
I felt that life was just starting.
I did on my own what I could
(At least, I hope I did).

I knew my friends well enough,
Much better than they did me,
And that was all that mattered anyway.
For any more was tough,
Any less made instability.
Anyway, nothing so trifling ever stood in my way.

There was one friend I knew much better
(Or so I thought) than others.
And as far as that person's mind was concerned,
I could predict his next move accurately, while others knew but
    little.
My position got no worse
Even as, one by one, each year passed.

But at the age of twelve, no less,
It seemed to me that destiny
Was pulling us farther and farther apart
And our friendship was that at best.
I thought, at times, it was rather funny,
That years together had made so much difference to my heart.

We both thought our worlds were ours alone,
Where dreams were never broken,
Values remained a charm.
But, for our oblivion, we had to atone,
And our joy had to be forsaken.
Happiness truly walks hand in hand with harm.

I spoke my mind freely,
Never hesitating in my speech,
While the latter, more reserved,
Thought that attempting to describe was silly,
And, soon out of my reach,
Was for ever engulfed in another world.

A world of money – the sovereign emperor,
Where dreams are broken for food.
And I watched sorry and helpless
As our worlds became worlds of terror;
All forsook good…
Just for the sake of their pointless quest.

Growing Up

Though maybe not in years,
But surely in mind,
Gone are childish tears,
That life I've left behind.
I could have gone on and on,
Never learning, never changing.
But now my early years have gone,
Their colours are gradually fading.
I always know what I am doing,
Of my actions I am aware,
Slowly I am learning
To help, to love, to care.
Gone are years of foolishness,
Yet memories ever a joy,
I know the meaning of true happiness;
My emotions are no longer a toy.
I feel the need to move forward,
I hate to waste my time,
Yet at each step my eyes are blurred,
As regret intones a chime.
I know what has to be done,
With that I greet each day...
The battle of the future must be won,
And my past will fade away.

Dreams – Their Reality

Dreams are sweet, but so untrue,
Their essence forever to lure,
To raise hopes and self-esteem,
If we can figure out what they really mean.

Underneath, when we are sleeping,
We can dream without any disturbing
Thoughts saying, 'This is wrong...
Faith in these will not last long.'

A person's character reflected deep inside,
Can only show what they are really like.
What are their innermost desires.
Ardent hopes and inspirers.

A person's thoughts during the day
And night are so far away,
And only those at night are true,
Yet, as premonitions, they are untrue.

What we really hope for,
Something never expressed before,
Known, maybe, not even to ourselves,
Will eventually express themselves.

Realising them can bring content,
Yet just visualising brings discontent.
But by making sure your aims are true,
You can make your dreams come true.

Grammar - A Complex Sentence

Life is full and yet empty,
You have all but you have none,
And where you feel you have plenty,
You find you have only one,
For at first (but not the very first)
You have all you think you need,
But as you grow up you thirst
For more, and you see you need
More things, and people and much more
Time to think, before we can say
Anything, for we lack confidence inside,
Though outside we put up a good show
And say we feel the world to be very wide,
But there again, we know,
Privacy is not to be found,
Anything said is contradicted,
Any thought ruled unsound,
And all acts convicted,
For this is the age of doubt and, more than
Anything, we need to be alone
To be able to find out where and when
To do what, and though we are prone
To make mistakes, only through them,
We can correct ourselves
And be prepared, for by then
Time has sped and we have to adjust ourselves,
To whatever is next to come,
To wonder again what went wrong,
To doubt again for years to come,
To be confused for ever so long.

Part 3
Confession

Mystery

There is a strange little truth behind every happening,
And, as always, it is harder to believe than a lie.
It is the same with me; there is a secret within me.
You may be the closest person I know, but even, my confidant being,
You will never touch one part of me,
One part of myself will never be free,
A little secret self that will, with me, die.

I find interest in others' emotions; not curiosity,
But mere interest as to their reactions and motives.
I feel now I can practically read another's mind
As if it were not them in that position, but me.
I am known for insouciance,
Yet, like the mystery I feel and know myself to be,
I am just the direct opposite.

I am not known for patience, but for strong will,
I live life enjoying each day,
I live not in tomorrow, nor in yesterday,
But in the mists of today, and, as if it were a priceless jewel,
I fondle it, and thrive in its secret depths.
For me, mystery is a necessity.
I am never satisfied, unless the solution I can safely and confidently say.

I love to wander far in my dreams,
Not into wild fantasies with no meaning,
But meaningful thoughts which seem important to me.
And yet, to me it seems,
Soaring with the powerful eagle to new horizons
Is no mesh to be entangled in either.
I guess I am, even to myself, too damn confusing.

Wonder After Wonder

This is an attempt at an explanation.
Beyond belief, I have learnt so much.
It is strange but in this world you can never say
How little or much you have learnt as such,
For little things varying in significance pass by each day,
Each brings a difference to our lives, our thoughts.
And beauty influences us to our extremes.
But in fact, even that is but one little affair
In the face of the magnitude of the universe.
Yet very few seem to know or care.
The biggest wonder to me is that
I've written many times, in many verses, many moods;
My pen has flown in ecstasy to different tunes
And never once has it stopped in its pursuit
Of the ultimate it wished to know.
Far away in my own world,
Lost in realms of fantasy,
Hardly present, a mere spectator to happiness and pain,
I would never, until now, play my own life's melody,
Through the heat of summer or the freshness of rain.
Outwardly perhaps I am playing
A funny game with a double identity,
For though I shared at times in the pleasures of society,
I preferred and prefer to be alone; by myself I am a unity
Pondering on reality, and the truths of divinity.
Surely at times I wondered,
'What the devil am I doing?
To the world I seem to be a youth, childish and sweet.
To myself, I feel I am more far-seeing;

To whom am I giving truth... to whom deceit?'
But after all, life is by itself
A strange thing where we seem to know so much
Yet in reality find we know so little.
In the midst of frauds like destiny and luck
Our life is insignificant, its existence brittle.
If only one could know all,
Could discover the secrets of immortality,
Could find an unscientific difference between life and death...
Could know the essence of divinity;
Could find the hidden secrets of the universe in his quest.
If only someone could unfurl
The curled lashings of the tides,
The nebulous gatherings in the heavens.
An impossibility, no less,
But at least I can wish.
That is the main reason I
Have no interest whatsoever in the wanderings of my mind.
In fact I hardly care, for it is only in a dream
That one can, in this world, have room to find
Solace, ironic though it may seem.
I prefer to be far away,
Where cold showers sprinkle my face,
Heavenly flowers adorn a pedestal.
Where am I? The Lord knows which place.
I seem to find my happiness somewhere after all,
But in a world like that of ours,
One cannot think of what may be
Only of what is.
It is AD 1995 –
    A Crazy World This Is.

Unfortunately

It is strange, for one truth I have tried
To discover for myself and I have found
Myself to be right and my idea sound,
But the more correct I prove myself to be,
The more the result sounds senseless and crazy.
It begins with a version of my own life –
An experience I can never seem to forget...
The more I try the more it gets set.
And the deeper I go into that subject
The more my analysis seems perfect.
A trivial thing as this should not
Usually inspire me,
But this seems to be
A slightly unusual case, where I feel I
Have uncovered a truth in the middle of a lie.
It probably makes no sense to you,
Possibly less than to me, but still
I can't help it; I simply feel
That this thought is as important as any...
For it is one among many.

A mere path life is, no doubt,
With no beginning and no end,
No short cut and no bend,
But within it is engulfed a number of years...
A variety of emotions, hopes and fears.
I am merely at the start,
Not even in teens I am named 'a kid'
But even I do and did
Have feelings about the world around me,
The workings and malfunctions of society.
I have not been watching
While others faced life's complexities.
I grew too, I did most of their activities.
But I realise that, while I was younger,
I wished for when I would grow older.
And now, though it may be strange,
I miss that stage of youth badly...
That innocence, that carefree love – yet sadly
I fear that will last no more...
It is prefixed with before.

Mad Desire

It was a clear night when,
I simply looked up to see,
Millions of stars dazzling and lovely.
I felt a strange sense of security
That I had never known before.
I think it was then
I realised the power of its beauty...
But was it only I
Who wished for an impossibility,
To possess this charm when it could never be mine...

Paradox

Words are my life;
My life is words.
Expressed with beauty,
Yet staying unheard.

Secret

Though in movies, people try their level best
With fogs, shades and moving mists
To create an obvious mood of mystery,
Through tricks and falsifying images from the wrist
They work to induce secrecy,
None of their works will ever come anywhere near
The absolutely obvious yet intricately covered
Secrecy of the man who has something to hide.

Come dark nights where the supposedly misty
Fog covers the full moon.
Instead, it is a mere crescent, the sky crystal-clear.
For no secret can change nature so soon,
Its value is never so dear.
My home, haven, each missing something;
I fret on my bed, aimlessly hoping
For the thing I wait for and yearn for to come to me.

Day's brightness does not make any difference.
Yet there is a comical touch to my day.
For when friends, inquisitive and supposing,
Yearn to trick me, to make me say
What it is for which I am waiting,
I ward away their queries with a mere "Nothing"
And though they lie that they agree, they know I am lying
And so the days pass in varying monotony.

They may wonder what it is for which I yearn,
Not out of care, but out of curiosity.
But I do not care, I work my way to my goal
Whether or not I am entitled to its quality.
But were they to know what I held behind, it would throw
Some into the depths of shock, some into disgust.
Others may congratulate me, feeling they must.
I don't care, I still wait through my clear nights, forever hoping,
    waiting...

In Another's Eyes

There is a depth in every woman.
Every hand that holds the child
Has a certain hold over the universe,
But none like this woman.
She is a lover of depth and mystery,
Of refined beauty based on wisdom,
Of passion which in no context is mild.

Her intent, analysing gaze is one that enthrals,
For she is no ordinary woman –
Perhaps in the light of cameras, yes,
But her glow is one that calls
For attention... she is
A secret, almost a sorceress;
In worldly affairs, she is no frightened kitten.

Though her temper moves to extremes, her love is devotional,
Though it is seldom transparent.
Nobody can love people more fiercely or purely
Or can make the world seem more beautiful.
Her eyes are rarely those that shake with tears.
Her eye has never profusely make a show.
Calm and stolid, her motives are never apparent.

She has a mystical sixth sense,
And a see-through point of view.
It looks like she almost can see
Into the misty future.
Her eyes bore into a mind intensely
And can read it clearly, because of her understanding
Of human nature; yet she interprets life at face value.

She seems interested only in philosophical wisdom;
Always drawn to the shadows, she knows what life is all about.
She has a strong yet secretive personality
And that can never be overcome.
In that deep refined countenance
She tries to be just and honest,
But her mystery secret life is strictly marked 'Private – Keep Out'.

Decision

"Blow on, blow harder," I urged the wind,
As tiny blasts of air
Blew into my hair,
Each lock wildly from my forehead unfurled,
As I stood and waited
Alone, as time abated,
But I felt I had all the time in the world.
If they called people dreamy,
Then I was in such a mood,
That 'alive' would be too good
A word to describe me –
For once, absolutely placid,
Instead of the usual
Violent self that all knew me to be.

I wondered, 'Am I what I
Suppose myself to be
Or is my true personality
Something much farther away?'
I had never thought
And had never been wrought
With a problem as crazy.
Generally I thought I was
The type, never perturbed,
Whom nothing disturbed
And no matter what the cause
Always stuck to a decision,
Usually a correct one,
And yet had an average number of flaws.

I wondered if the dame next door
Also thought the same,
That is, if she knew my name,
And also if the people on the top floor
Paid as much attention to me
As they did to their future, but I'm sure,
At that rate, they'd be at death's door.
Did I have ambitions?
Yes, if you can call
Them that at all,
For I only wished to better all opposition,
But as for me alone
There wasn't much I had done.
(That was a depressing observation.)

I have, I feel, the capacity to admire,
To love or hate something passionately,
To speak foolishly or sincerely,
And I decided that just standing there
Was both foolish and useless,
While being absolutely senseless.
Slowly, I moved from my lair.
I looked at my watch; it had been
But a few seconds since
But now I felt it was a sin
To wait there, for it seemed
I had a road to follow,
I had no time now,
And, crossing the road, I left the scene.

The Truth At Last

Not for me high aspirations and desires,
Not for me heights of heroism and fame,
My feelings for life are those for a game.
Such a heart is mine.

Not for me reality, its haste and sham,
Not for me lies and trickery,
My feelings are of tranquillity.
Such a heart is mine.

Not for me sensitivity or stolidity,
Not for me compassion –
My feelings are of passion.
Such a heart is mine.

Not for me false quietude,
Not for me; I confess that
My feelings are those of a poet.
Such a heart is mine.

Part 4

A Bit of Advice

Road To Happiness

Among all haste there is placidity,
Amidst all commotion lies serenity.

Life can be lies and trickery
And also virtue and simplicity.

Know yourself, your feelings and limits,
Hope not while living for eternal bliss.

Be yourself, hold that a talisman.
Amidst emotions was created man.

Look not above or down below,
The secrets of life hope not to know.

Do not go beyond your capacity,
Never rise in lividity.

Nothing can truly be counted on to last.
Life moves slowly, time moves fast.

The best of fortunes can change its course.
As the gentlest breezes can change their force.

Trust not money, nor fame.
But in the world make good your name.

Think not of torture, deceit or trickery,
Yet live not in imaginations and fantasy.

Vast is the mind, dwell on its power.
Live not on others, work by the hours.

Beauty is found where you look for it,
Music is heard when you wish to hear it.

Watch sunsets if you wish, but build no castles in the air.
Rely on God; work hard, leave not life to prayer.

Use Time, make it bow to your will.
But remember, you can never make running water still.

The forces of nature were born earlier.
Likewise, take examples from the older and wiser.

Love not youth, but enjoy its freedom.
When you lose it, sink not into boredom.

Live in purity, simplicity and truth,
From the moment in the world you set foot.

Do not thrive on winnings, yet never feel defeated:
Nobody always gets only one, rest assured.

Go through life's noises not closing your ears.
But hearing its pitiful sounds burst not into tears.

Help others, but do not leave them to ruin you.
In a world of money, no friend is true.

Do not fear the world, gain confidence.
For its virtue, save your reverence.

Think, if you cannot tell right from wrong,
But on thinking, do not be long.

Be your own judge, jury and master.
On your destiny do not ponder.

Your future is coming to you day by day;
And from it you can't run away.

Simple Advice, Hard To Follow

Be yourself when you're new around;
It's you that people like.

Be yourself when people tire of you
But be sure of each step you take.

Be yourself if people hate you,
Only change the bad side.

Be yourself if you want to be loved,
What counts is the inside.

Be yourself if you're popular,
It's your true self they'll like.

Be yourself if it means nothing to you,
What difference will it make!

Be yourself if you stand to lose,
There's still something to gain.

Be yourself if you've lost all hope,
Then try winning again.

Be yourself if it's peaceful,
It makes you fit to reign.

Be yourself if it's stormy,
You'll rule the terrain.

Be yourself and you'll see in time,
Your luck will be ordained

Be yourself and you'll see the difference,
And your self-esteem will remain.

Sadly...

A voice can be heard by all,
Yet few wish to hear.
The unheard endure it all,
And live on, year after year.

Absolute Contentment

What is the spirit,
The essence of life?
Is it the triumph
Of accomplishment and strife?

Or is it beauty;
Dashing splendour and glory,
Natural beauty with the satisfaction it brings,
Or is such contentment all a story?

Material things are of no value,
For never do they last,
Nor does anyone envy it for long...
Such satisfaction goes fast!

It could be a wonderful personality,
Or some kind of talent,
I cannot say for sure,
But the list of possibilities never ends!

Self-Esteem

If you find you don't have something
That many others do,
Just read onwards
And you'll know what to do.
When such a thing happens,
Think of something else,
Like what you have that others don't;
Such a thought really helps.

Your friends may feel the same way:
They look for things in you
That they feel they don't have;
It's a natural attitude.
What you have may be material
Or perhaps a talent.
Whatever it is, be proud of it
That's where your problem ends.

God Helps Those Who Help Themselves

Turning to Krishna's idol,
I asked it to foresee,
To touch my crystal ball,
And here's what it told me...

"My job's to play the flute,
Not the future to see,
But which tune you plan to toot,
Is up to you, not me."

Judge Yourself

If an evil deed makes you lose your self-esteem,
Then look over the years,
Ignorant though your act may seem,
It still brings some tears.

Each good deed done in the past,
Each wonderful moment,
Each achievement, first and last,
Each friend who went.

Think of the good that you have done,
Sylvan forests you have crossed,
Each difficulty you've overcome;
Each minute that has passed.

Believe me, I too know:
I've done both good and evil,
But looking back, as I do now,
I'm regaining my former will.

Part 5
Eulogy

I Agree, But Not For Me

Oh, Lord! Strange are your ways,
Futile are and futile will remain
My attempts to define or explain
Your absolute craze
To bend others to your will
And at the same time still
Allow others to defy you.
Each of my explanations proves untrue.
Me, you'll never cease to amaze.

You set others' fates and destiny.
Yes, even relentless destiny bows
To your wishes. And it vows
To carry out your necessity.
And yet you never tire,
Or cease to admire
The absolute impeccable imperfectness
That your creations achieve in their laziness.
In their cases, of course, their fate is your felicity.

You managed to create
In the world hunger,
Pain and anger,
And their toll will never abate.
Yet even during their
Horrifying reign here
You managed to instil within some
Contentment, pleasure, happiness and even nauseating boredom.
But it is none of these which helps me to write.

Vision of Loveliness

Her words are music,
Her voice a tune,
Her life may be tragic
But her heart's immune.
Her strength unmatched,
She reigns above,
Her power unquestioned,
The power of love.
Her feet a delicate flower,
Yet her pace incredible;
Fresh of face like an early rain shower;
Hands versatile and capable.
She walks on the earth,
While the universe watches in awe.
As elemental as the dirt,
Features refined, yet raw.
Stars shine above her head.
Flowers adorn her hair.
She lies in a lovely flower bed,
Singing a soft melodious prayer.

Dreams and hopes form her life,
Her songs a gift to all.
To live her ambitions forever she strives,
Standing straight and tall;
Never a slouch in her graceful walk,
Her head ever held high.
Never impatience or rudeness in talk,
Never in speech a lie.
Her words pleasant to all around,
Not a word is indiscreet,
Her voice never the only sound
Her tone is always sweet.
Not a thing is for herself,
Though her life may be her own.
Her words never contain the word 'self'.
Her talents untold, yet shown.
Her beauty is not of eyes or looks,;
Her strength comes from within;
Her features are not found in books,
Her origin in heaven.

This loveliness lies for ever,
Her strength lives on much longer,
Forever, they make people stay together,
Making friendliness linger.
There's not a thing she doesn't know,
Her wit has no equal;
Her heart lies with all below:
Her love is for all.
All friendly, she has none to hate,
Neither lady nor man,
There is one point on which there is no debate –
She is the perfect woman.

Bapu – An Ideal Idol

Bapu! You've given us
The perfect way to be,
The right direction to go
And an angle through which to see
How life is going to be,
How we want it to go,
The difference between the two,
And how little of it we know.

Our ideals, set by you,
Should contain tolerance,
Concern, courage, and determination,
And their life-long maintenance.
And today we take this oath,
To sever the bad in us,
To bring in truth at all costs,
And we hope God will be with us.

Part 6
The Sands of Time

Memories

If life were a sandy beach
On which danced wave upon wave,
Some lashy and strong,
Others milder, and suave,
Yet their effects lasting long.

Some touching, barely,
A sweet, gentle tingling,
The warmth of the sun,
At times, yet divine in their being.
In real life, we call that fun.

Each salty streak falling
At our feet, we remember later
And, in our life, each event
We think of it after
It has gone, wondering,
Whence it was sent.

Ten Years From Now

This house was somewhere in my past,
I can feel some attachment.
These dark walls, lived in by another now,
Are in a sorry predicament.
Whose fault? I doubt if I know.
This road holds some memories.
I can almost see
Myself, carefree, a mere child.
No matter how different its looks are going to be,
This road's value is by no means mild.
These white fences resplendent
More in pride than beauty.
It deserves reverence, for, like us,
It has felt the passing of years.
For better or for worse –
There is joy in a family album;
Surely this is not me;
I never ran and played in the mud.
But, then again, it could be.
My past seems so far; like an age has passed
But come, you can't expect me
To actually believe
That this kid on the left is now that famous doctor.

But even I seem to have been
In another world, pursuing only career.
The height matrix is truly untrue.
I could never have been four feet two.
But then, all else seems to be nuts.
This may be quite possible too;
Heaven help me!
I want to go back ten years – Fast!

Time – A Fleeting Glimpse

The past is gone and far away,
The present is with us,
It's the latter we care about,
Though it isn't in our hands.

The present seems to slip away
And become the past.
Without warning it leaves us,
You can't catch time – it moves so fast!

The present we try and remember,
When it has become past,
With tenderness we think of it
Though it is gone and past!

With fear we attend to future,
With the unknown we are lost,
Exciting and disappointing,
Unpredictable till the last!

Past is unforgettable,
Present is never there,
The future is a wonderful dream.
Hope it comes true, then and there!

Pandora and Life

If I took the future, present and past,
To be a corridor...
In order of time as first and last,
Future would be behind a locked door.

Hardly one among a thousand
Would dare to unlock it,
Take their destiny by the hand
And never flinch at it.

Many may feel they want to know,
And place by the door their ear...
Or peep at the light below
Yet are afraid it is not what they wish to hear.

The future is best unknown,
The suspense best felt,
Worry is never to be shown,
It is never well meant.

Part 7
Denouement

Writing Poetry

It is not at all
A question of capability,
But of a small
Bit of tranquillity.
Either a deserted balcony,
Where the sun rises at dawn,
With indescribable beauty,
Indicating the morn,
Or even a lone window,
Where satin rain drips and falls;
Where time is slow,
And almost seems to stall;
To find words from nowhere,
To be lost in another world,
To find rhyme and verse,
And jot them down, word by word.

Where Words Are Useless

A person may feel in time,
The greatest happiness,
The worst of sadness,
Yet even these can words express.

The greatest humour can be in rhyme,
The utmost of boredom,
Can in words come,
As can any of the worst or best.

Moments that felt sour as lime,
Bitterness and anger,
All pain and hunger,
Can in words for ever rest.

But some moments do in life arrive,
When the pen cannot describe,
Nor can the best scribe,
And they only in memory exist.

It Is Much More

It is more than the soul,
Much more than the spirit
That encourages a poet
To write.
Each and every person makes
A part of a poet's stakes.

Part 8
Experience

- A good sportsman treats wins and losses the same way.
- A dreamer dreams to do, a doer does his dreams.
- Count your age when you realise its value.
- All have brains. Few use them.
- A good winner wins with the worst deal.
- Your luck is as good or bad as you make it for yourself.
- Nothing we own is truly ours except our character.
- Truth cannot be measured. What is said is either a truth or a lie.
- Desire is a result of envy.
- Pain is a result of anger.
- To realise your dreams you have to wake up.
- A true friend never boasts that he is one.
- A good song is felt, not heard.
- A liar always says he tells the truth.
- If you want something badly enough, you'll get it.
- Worry causes more worry.
- A calm mind can rule the world.
- Millions can read, few understand.
- Music fills the heart; a heart is felt in music.
- Never limit your capacity, but know your limits.
- All sounds are music, but to whose ears is the question.
- The dead are at peace with the world yet nobody wants this peace.

- He is happy who is reconciled to his fate.
- You get only what you deserve.
- It is pointless to try the pointless.
- By looking for your destiny, you are making it.
- Never let others decide for you what you can decide for yourself.
- At times, the forces of nature bow down to aspirations, but they never relent in mercy to despair.
- It is never wrong to look at the right; it is never right to look at the wrong.
- The weakest man is he who trips, even over grass.
- He is at peace with himself who is at peace with others.
- He who is afraid of others is afraid of himself.
- The strength of man lies not only in his ability to bow before the right people but also in his ability to judge who they are.
- He is unhappy who feels it is his right to be so for the simple yet illogical reason that others have made him feel that way.
- Perhaps beauty is in the eyes of the seer, but its praise lies only in his words.
- Life is logically simple, yet practically difficult.
- It is easier to watch others do something than to do it yourself.
- The only thing worse than thinking too much of yourself is thinking too little.
- He is remarkably eloquent who can define emotions precisely without feeling them himself.
- Loneliness is just a state of mind.

- Wealth is a matter of opinion, not comparison.
- Versatility is not always quality.
- A lie can contain a grain of truth, but in truth there is no place for a lie.
- If something has to end it has to begin.
- Count your gains by subtracting the losses.
- Pain comes only during those few moments when we do not attempt to forget or ignore it.
- An axiom is something that neither can be proven right nor can it be proven wrong.
- There is no place in a logical thinker's mind for superlatives.
- Things can only be judged by their impact on our lives.
- A man's worst enemy is himself.
- Silence is the voice of the unheard.
- Poets and scientists will always remain each others' critics.